Jump!

Written by
Stephen Rickard

This frog likes to jump.

It likes to jump over the balls.

This penguin likes to jump.
It likes to jump on to the ice.

This dog likes to jump.
It likes to jump to catch the ball.

This whale likes to jump.

It likes to jump to make a big splash.

This rabbit likes to jump.
It likes to jump over the fence.

We like to jump.
We like to jump into the water.

We like to jump.
We like to jump out of the plane.

We like to jump.
We like to jump off a high tower.

We don't like to jump.
We don't like to walk.
We like to sleep.